AUTHOR

TITLE   KNOW THE GAME,   SOCCER

CLASSIFICATION NO.   796.334

ACCESSION NO.   084598

officials are referred to individually as
'he'. This should, of course, be taken
to mean 'he or she' where appropriate.

Penalty kick 40

Contents

The game 2

Equipment 2
Players' equipment 2
Footwear 4
Ball 5

Field of play 6
Boundary lines 8
Centre circle 8
Technical area 9
Penalty area 10
Penalty arc 10
Goal area 11
Flag posts 11

The match 13
Start and restart of pl:
Duration of the game
Suspension of play 14
Substitution 14
Scoring a goal. 14

1

The game

A game of soccer is played between two teams of not more than 11 players. One of each team must be the goalkeeper. Each team attempts to score goals and the team scoring the greater number of goals is the winner.

Acknowledgements

The publishers would like to thank Umbro International, Mitre Sports and Nike for their photographic contributions to this book.

Photographs on inside front and inside back covers and pages 4 and 47 courtesy of Allsport UK. Photographs on front and back covers and pages 3, 18, 25, 27, 28 and 39 courtesy of Empics.

Illustrations by Dave Saunders.

Equipment

Players' equipment

The usual equipment of a player consists of jersey or shirt, shorts, socks, footwear and shin guards.

Players must ensure that their shin guards are completely covered by their socks at all times.

While there are no specific size requirements in the Laws of the Game concerning shin guards, they must provide a reasonable degree of protection. They may be made of rubber, plastic, polyurethane or any similar substance.

A player should not wear anything which may cause injury to another player or himself. He may wear spectacles at his own risk and at the discretion of the referee.

Teams should be distinguished from each other (and from the referee) by the colours they wear, while goalkeepers have to be recognisable as such by wearing colours different from those of the other players and the referee.

Visible undergarments such as thermopants (cycling shorts) are allowed. They must, however, be of the same predominant colour as the shorts of the player's team and they must not extend beyond the top of the knee. (If a team wears multi-coloured shorts, the undergarments must be of the same colour as the shorts' predominant colour.)

Some leagues have a compulsory ruling that the players must wear numbers on the backs of their shirts or jerseys.

▲ Shin guards

If a player is found to have any item of personal equipment not conforming to these requirements, he must leave the field at the referee's request, to remedy the fault. The referee will instruct the player to leave the field to correct his equipment, if he has not already done so, when the ball next goes out of play. The player cannot return without first reporting to the referee, who has to satisfy himself that the player's kit is in order. The player may only enter the field at a moment when the ball has ceased to be in play.

▼ Goalkeeper's gloves

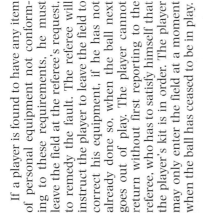

Footwear

Footwear is an essential part of a player's equipment. Much experimentation has been carried out to produce footwear suited to individual requirements, and yet conforming to regulations. The lightweight boot, because it allows comfort and lightness of touch, is now much preferred to the heavy and more durable type.

A player is responsible for ensuring that his footwear is not dangerous to another player.

Ball

The ball must be spherical and have an outer casing of leather or another material approved by the International Board. Nothing used in its construction should pose a danger to players.

The soccer ball must be 68–70 cm (27–8 in) in circumference, and at the start of the game its weight must be 410–50 g (14–16 oz). The pressure of the ball must be equal to 0.6–1.1 atm. which equals 600–1100g/sq cm (8.5–15.6 lb/sq in) at sea level.

Soccer balls with a waterproofed surface can now be obtained: this means that the weight will remain approximately the same throughout a game, even on wet and muddy grounds. A white waterproofed ball is easier to see than a dark one on winter days. The ball can only be changed during the game with the consent of the referee.

For games played by schoolchildren on artificial pitches, balls with protected seams are available. A size 3 or 4 is usually recommended for primary and lower secondary school children.

Field of play

The size of the playing field may have an important bearing on play. Because of possible difficulties in obtaining adequate playing spaces, the Laws of the Game allow limited variation in dimensions, but stipulate that the length must always exceed the width. Internal markings are, however, always constant. Clubs should try to obtain a field which conforms to the dimensions for international matches: maximum 110 x 75 m (120 x 80 yds), minimum 100 x 64 m (110 x 70 yds).

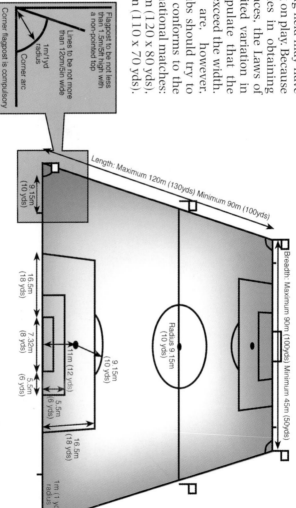

Flagpost to be not less than 1.5m/5ft high with a non-pointed top

Lines to be not more than 12cm/5in wide

1m/1yd radius

Corner arc

Corner flagpost is compulsory

Length: Maximum 120m (130yds) Minimum 90m (100yds)

Breadth: Maximum 90m (100yds) Minimum 45m (50yds)

9.15m (10 yds)

16.5m (18 yds)

7.32m (8 yds)

11m (12 yds)

5.5m (6 yds)

5.5m (6 yds)

16.5m (18 yds)

Radius 9.15m

9.15m (10 yds)

1m (1 yd) radius

▶ *Fig.1 Size of the field of play; although not strictly accurate, 1 yd is accepted as the imperial equivalent of 1 m.*

It is in the best interests of the game to secure and maintain, by effective draining and careful upkeep, a good, level field of grass. Where there is a need for continual daily practice on a pitch, it may be advisable to lay down a porous 'all-weather' surface instead of turf.

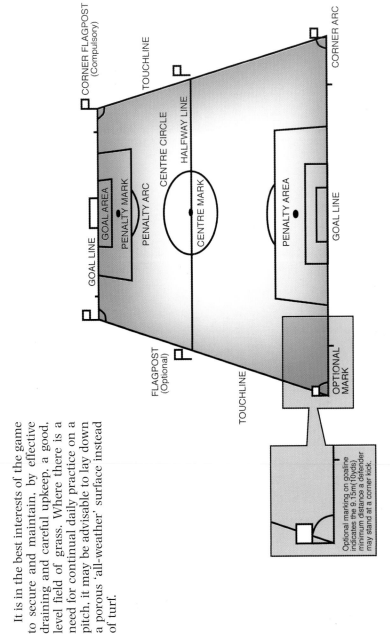

▲ *Fig.2 The field of play*

Optional marking on goaline indicates the 9.15m(10yds) minimum distance a defender may stand at a corner kick.

Boundary lines

Touch lines

These are the longer boundary lines. When the ball passes wholly over them it is out of play. Play is then re-started with a throw-in.

Goal lines

Goal lines are the lines at each end of the field, joining and at right angles to the touch lines. The width of a goal line must be the same as the depth of the goal posts and cross-bar. When the whole of the ball passes over the goal line (except between the goal posts and under the cross-bar, when a goal is scored), either on the ground or in the air, the ball is out of play and the game is re-started by:

● a goal kick (when the ball has last been played by or touched an attacking player)

● a corner kick (when the ball has last been played by or touched a defending player).

Note Touch lines and goal lines are part of the field of play, just as all markings are part of the area they enclose.

Halfway line

This indicates a division of the field into two equal halves for the purpose of:

● the kick-off – when all the players must remain in their own half of the field until the kick-off has been taken

● offside – a player cannot be offside if he is in his own half of the field at the moment the ball is played by a member of his own team.

Centre circle

Together with the penalty arc, this provides a practical indication of the law that *for all forms of free kick, the players of the offending side shall be at least 9.15 m (10 yds) from the ball and shall not approach within 9.15 m (10 yds) until the kick has been taken. Note: the above law applies to offending players standing behind the ball as well as those in front of it, except in three cases:*

● for a penalty kick, all players, other than the goalkeeper and the kicker, must be outside the penalty area, within the field of play, behind the ball, and at least 9.15 m from the ball at the time the kick is taken; the goalkeeper must remain on his goal line, between the goal posts

● at a goal kick, all attacking players must be outside the penalty area

● when an indirect free kick is awarded against a side in its own penalty area but less than 9.15 m (10 yds) from goal, defending players may stand on their own goal line between the goal posts; otherwise they must not be less than 9.15 m (10 yds) from the ball.

Technical area

At most grounds, particularly where a high level of football is played, there are technical areas around the team benches. These may extend 1 m to the side of the dugout and must stop at least 1 m from the touch line.

A team official may leave his position on the bench and use the technical area to give instructions to the team. He must then return to his position.

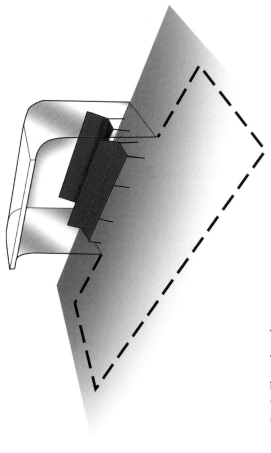

▲ *Fig. 3 The technical area*

Penalty area

This is a rectangle 40.3 x 16.5 m (44 x 18 yds), including the width of the lines. It serves the following purposes:

• it indicates that part of the field in which, for any of the ten 'penal' offences (*see* page 20) committed by a defending player, a penalty kick is awarded

• it indicates the part of the field of play where the ball may be handled by the defending goalkeeper

• it indicates the area beyond which the ball must be kicked for it to be in play from a goal kick or from a free kick awarded to the defending side in its own penalty area

• when a penalty kick is awarded, it indicates the area outside which all players, other than the goalkeeper and the player taking the penalty kick, must be, or outside which all opposing players must remain while a goal kick or free kick is taken by the defending side.

Penalty mark

For a penalty kick the ball is placed on the penalty mark, which is sited inside the penalty area at a point 11 m (12 yds) from the centre of the goal line and at a right angle to it.

Penalty arc

The penalty arc is not part of the penalty area. By being 9.15 m (10 yds) from the penalty mark and outside the penalty area, it indicates the additional area into which encroachment is not permitted when a penalty kick is being taken.

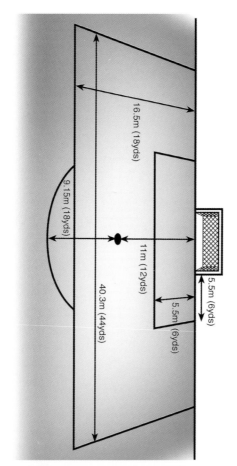

▶ *Fig. 4   The penalty area and the goal area*

Goal area

The goal area is the area in which the ball is placed for a goal kick.

For a goal kick the ball can be placed anywhere in the goal area. Many goal-keepers place the ball near the forward corners of the goal area, perhaps because such a position adds a little distance to their kick, or allows them a convenient run (but most likely because it is the accustomed position). If the ball were placed a little away from the extreme corners, it might afford better footing at the time the kick is made.

Goals

The width and depth of the goal posts and cross-bar must not exceed 12 cm (5 in). They must be square, rectangular, round or elliptical in shape.

The goal mouth itself measures 7.32 m (8 yds) between goal posts and 2.44 m (8 ft) from the ground to the lower edge of the cross-bar.

The goal posts and the cross-bar may only be made of wood or metal. They must be white.

While their use is advised, nets are not compulsory except under the rules of certain competitions. They should be properly pegged down and fastened to the back of the goal posts and bars so that they are not hazardous to the goalkeeper. Wire mesh is not permitted, as it is danger-ous to players.

Publicity of any kind is not allowed on the field, the goal posts, goal nets or corner flags.

These must be firmly fixed but not too rigid, or they may cause injury if a player collides with them. They may not be removed or inclined to assist a player who is taking a kick.

Corner flag posts must not be less than 1.5 m (5 ft) high, and must not be pointed at the top. They mark the corners, and assist the officials in deciding whether a ball passing close to the corner has gone over the touch line or the goal line.

Halfway flag posts are not essential, but if used they must be opposite the halfway line and not less than 1 m (1 yd) outside the touch line.

Flag posts

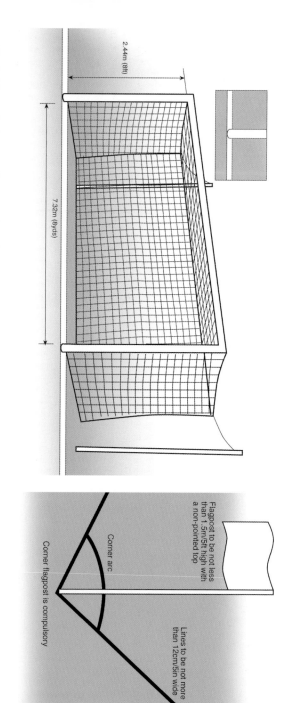

2.44m (8ft)

7.32m (8yds)

Flagpost to be not less than 1.5m/5ft high with a non-pointed top

Corner arc

Corner flagpost is compulsory

Lines to be not more than 12cm/5in wide

▶ Fig.5   The goal: the inset illustrates how the width of the goal line must be the same as the depth of the goal post and cross-bar.

▶ Fig.6   The corner flag post

The match

Start and restart of play

It is customary for the captains of the two teams to shake hands with the referee and each other before the game starts, and then for the home captain to toss a coin, giving the visiting captain the call. The captain winning the toss may choose which goal his team will defend in the first half. The other team take the kick-off to start the match.

For the kick-off, the ball is placed in a stationary position on the centre mark. When the referee gives the signal, a player from the team kicking off takes the kick-off.

Kick-off

Every player must remain in his own half of the field until the ball is in play. Players from the team that is not kicking off must be at least 9.15 m (10 yds) from the ball until it is in play.

The ball must be kicked into the opponents' half of the field, and is in play when it has been kicked and moves. The kicker must not play the ball a second time until it has touched or been played by another player. If he does, and the game has otherwise correctly started, an indirect free kick is awarded to the opposing side. For any other infringements of the law concerning the start of play, the kick-off is re-taken.

A goal can be scored direct from a kick-off. When a goal is scored, the game is re-started with a kick-off by the team conceding the goal.

After half-time, ends are changed and the game is re-started by the opposite team to that which kicked off in the first half. When extra time is necessary, the captains again toss for choice of end.

Duration of the game

The game is divided into two equal periods, each lasting 45 minutes, unless competition rules permit a reduction in each half. The half-time period must be stated in competition rules and may not exceed 15 minutes. It cannot be altered without the consent of the referee.

In certain competitions the rules specify the normal time and extra time (which may be necessary in the case of a drawn game) to be played. The length of the interval between the end of normal playing time and the start of extra time is at the discretion of the referee. The referee and players must abide by these rules and regulations.

In all games a referee is empowered to: make allowances (at his discretion) in either half of the game for time lost through substitution, removal from the field of injured players, time-wasting or other cause. He must extend time to permit a penalty kick to be taken.

13

Suspension of play

If play is stopped for an infringement of the laws, the game is started by an appropriate free kick.

In certain cases, play may be suspended for a cause not specifically mentioned in the laws. Examples are as follows:

• when play has been suspended because of injury to a player or official
• when the ball becomes lodged between two players and the situation may cause injury
• interference by a spectator or other outside agent, causing the game to be stopped
• when the ball bursts.

Provided the ball has not passed out of play immediately prior to the suspension, the referee re-starts the game by dropping the ball at its position when play was suspended. The ball is in play when it touches the ground; if a player touches the ball before it reaches the ground it must be re-dropped.

Should the ball have passed out of play immediately prior to suspension, the game is re-started by the appropriate method, e.g. goal kick, throw-in, etc.

Time lost through stoppages should be kept to a minimum by players and officials.

Substitution

In league or cup games the laws allow each side to use no more than three substitutes. Competition rules must state how many substitutes (maximum of seven) may be nominated. The names of substitutes must be given to the referee before the start of the match. If the game is a 'friendly' (i.e. one not played in a competition), there is no limit to the number of substitutes per team, provided that the agreed figure is given to the referee before the game.

During a stoppage in the game, a goalkeeper or any other player may be replaced, providing the referee is informed that a substitution is to be made. If he is not informed, the referee has to caution the players who infringe this law.

The referee also cautions a player who, after the game has started, enters or re-enters the field of play to join his team without the referee's permission. Similarly, a player must be cautioned if he leaves the field of play without the referee's consent (except when he leaves in the normal course of play).

Scoring a goal

For a goal to be scored, the whole of the ball must pass over the whole of the goal line, between the posts and under the cross-bar.

The ball must not be thrown, carried or propelled by the hand or arm of an attacking player, except in the case of a goalkeeper from his own penalty area.

If a defending player handles the ball and it passes over the line into the goal, a goal is scored. Should a goal be prevented by a defending player (other than the goalkeeper) handling the ball, a direct free kick is awarded to the attacking side; or if the offence occurred in the penalty area, a penalty kick is awarded. If a goal is prevented in either of these cases, the defending player is sent off the field and shown a red card.

A goal cannot be scored from an indirect free kick unless the ball has touched or been played by a second player of either team (other than the kicker) before passing into the goal.

If, when taking an indirect free kick, a player kicks directly into his opponents' goal, a goal kick is awarded to the defending team.

If a defender taking either a direct or an indirect free kick from outside his penalty area kicks into his own goal, a corner kick is awarded to the attacking team. Similarly, from a direct free kick a goal can only be scored directly against the offending side.

Deciding the result of drawn matches

In some competitions it is necessary to determine a winner to qualify for the next round or win a trophy. Extra time, usually 15 minutes each way, is often used for this purpose. Even then a result is not always obtained. FIFA has therefore approved two other methods of identifying a winner.

The Golden Goal

This is a special modification of extra time. As soon as a goal is scored by either team in extra time, the game ends and that team becomes the winner.

If a result is still not achieved, the winner can be determined by the taking of kicks from the penalty mark.

Kicks from the penalty mark

This can be used following extra time, with or without the Golden Goal option. Or it can be included in Competition Rules as a substitute for extra time. The referee decides which goal to use and the captains toss a coin, with the winning team taking the first kick. The teams take kicks in turn for up to 5 kicks each until a winner is determined. If both teams have used their free kicks and the scores are still level, the teams continue to take kicks in turn until a winner is determined after each team has taken the same number of kicks. Each player can only take one kick until everyone has had a turn.

A team whose opponents have less than 11 players at the end of the game or extra time names a number of its players who will not take kicks. This makes it fairer for them if the game reaches the stage where players have to take a second kick.

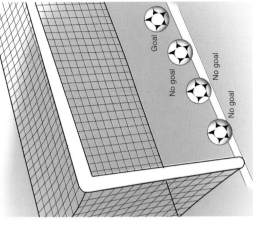

▲ *Fig.7 Scoring a goal*

15

Ball in and out of play

The markings on the ground are within the field of play, the outer edge being the true boundary line. The ball is out of play when it has wholly crossed the goal line or touch line in the air or on the ground.

Unless the ball goes completely over the goal lines or touch lines, it is not out of play if it rebounds from the referee (or assistant referee) when he is in the field of play. If it rebounds into the field of play from a goal post, cross-bar or corner flag post, it is still in play.

If a ball passes out of play during its flight, but swerves or is blown so that it falls in the field of play, a throw-in, goal kick or corner kick is given.

It is possible for the ball to be out of play when a player plays it or goal-keeper catches it, even though he is standing in the playing area. However, a player running outside the playing area may still keep the ball in play.

If a goalkeeper comes out of the penalty area and dives to handle the ball, part of his body may be on the ground outside it, although the ball is clearly in the penalty area when handled. It is the position of the ball which counts in cases such as this.

▼ *Fig.8 The ball is out of play when it has wholly crossed the goal line or touch line in the air or on the ground*

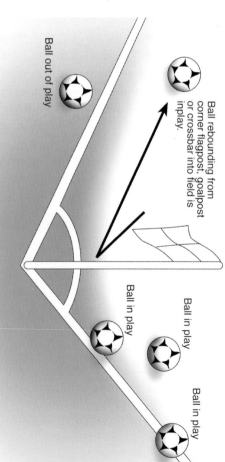

Ball out of play

Ball rebounding from corner flagpost, goalpost or crossbar into field is inplay.

Ball in play

Ball in play

Ball in play

Throw-in

If the ball goes out of play by passing wholly over the touch line, either on the ground or in the air, it is thrown in *from the point where it crossed the line.*

The following points relate to the throw-in:

• the throw-in is taken by an opponent of the player who last played or was last touched by the ball before it went out of play

• at the moment of delivering the ball, the thrower must face the field of play

• at the moment of delivering the ball, part of each foot must be on the ground, either on or outside the touch line. A player may raise his heels or drag his foot in making a throw. An infringement occurs if the thrower raises his heels so that part of his foot (or feet) is in the field of play without being in contact with the touch line

• the thrower must use both hands. It is wrong to throw in the ball with one hand, even if the other is touching or guiding the ball

• the thrower must deliver the ball from behind and over his head. Players can make certain that there is no doubt by taking the ball well over and behind the head, before throwing in. It is sometimes wrongly assumed that the player must release the ball while his hands are over his head. In a natural throwing movement, the hands will always be in front of the vertical plane of the body when the ball is released. The throw starts from behind the head and there should then be a continuous movement to the point of release

• the ball is in play immediately it is thrown and it passes over the touch line

• the thrower must not play the ball until it has been touched or played by another player. If he does so, an indirect free kick is taken by an opponent, from the place where the infringement occurred

• a goal cannot be scored direct from a throw-in

• a throw-in taken from any position other than the point where the ball passed over the touch line shall be considered to have been improperly thrown in

• if the ball is improperly thrown in, the throw-in is re-taken by a player of the opposing team

• a player cannot be offside direct from a throw-in

• the ball must be thrown, not dropped

• if the ball touches the ground before entering the field of play, the throw must be re-taken

• a goalkeeper cannot receive the ball directly into his hands from a throw-in taken by a player in his team.

Goal kick

If the ball goes wholly over the goal line but not into goal, and last touched or was played by a player of the attacking side, a goal kick is awarded to the defenders. The kick is taken from any point within the goal area.

The ball is not in play until it has passed into that part of the field of play beyond the penalty area. Should it not be kicked directly beyond the limit, the kick is re-taken. Players of the opposing side must remain outside the penalty area until the ball has been kicked beyond it.

A goalkeeper cannot receive the ball into his hands direct from a goal kick in order that he may thereafter kick it into play. When the ball has passed outside the penalty area, the kicker may not play the ball a second time before it has touched or been played by another player. Should he do so, an indirect free kick is awarded at the place where the infringement occurred, subject to the special

circumstances described below. A goal can be scored direct from a goal kick but only against the opposing team.

To encourage a rapid re-start of the game, the defender should be allowed to take the kick as soon as possible.

Special circumstances

• A free kick awarded to the defending team inside its own goal area is taken from any point within the goal area.

• An indirect free kick awarded to the attacking team in its opponents' goal area is taken from the goal area line parallel to the goal line at the point nearest to where the infringement occurred.

• A dropped ball to restart the match after play has been temporarily stopped inside the goal area takes place on the goal area line parallel to the goal line at the point nearest to where the ball was located when play was stopped.

Corner kick

A corner kick is awarded to the attacking team when the whole of the ball, having last touched or last been played by one of the defending team, passes over the goal line either on the ground or in the air (except when it goes into the goal).

The corner kick is taken by a player of the attacking team, the ball being placed inside the quarter circle at the corner flag post which is nearest to the point where the ball crossed over the line. The ball is 'inside' the quarter circle if it is wholly within, or overlaps any part of it.

The corner flag post must not be moved or removed for the kick to be taken.

A goal may be scored direct from a corner kick but only against the opposing team.

Players of the opposing team must not approach within 9.15 m (10 yds) of the ball until it is in play, i.e. until it has been kicked and it moves.

The player taking the corner kick must not play the ball a second time until it has been touched or played by another player. Should he do so, an indirect free kick is taken by a player of the opposing team from the place where the infringement occurred, subject to the special circumstances (*see* page 18).

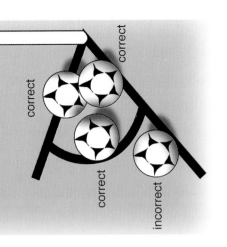

Fig.9 Placement of ball at corner kick: the ball must be within or overlap any part of the quarter circle ▲

Offences

Direct free kick offences

There are ten specific offences for which a player is penalised by the award of a direct free kick to the opposing side. If the offence is committed in the player's own penalty area, a penalty kick is awarded to the opponents.

A direct free kick is awarded if a player commits any of the following six offences in a manner considered by the referee to be careless, reckless or involving excessive force:

- charges an opponent
- pushes an opponent
- strikes or attempts to strike an opponent
- kicks or attempts to kick an opponent
- trips or attempts to trip an opponent
- jumps at an opponent

or if a player commits any of the following four offences:

- when tackling an opponent, makes contact with the opponent before contact is made with the ball
- spits at an opponent
- holds an opponent
- handles the ball deliberately (except in the case of a goalkeeper who handles the ball when it is in his own penalty area).

▲ *Fig.10   Kicking an opponent*

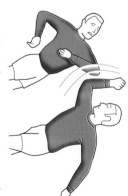

▲ *Fig.11   Striking or attempting to strike an opponent*

Indirect free kick offences

Some offences are penalised by the award of an indirect free kick against the offending side. These offences are:

- playing in a manner considered by the referee to be dangerous
- when not playing the ball, impeding the progress of an opponent (i.e. running between the opponent and the ball, or interposing the body so as to form an obstacle to the opponent)
- preventing the goalkeeper from releasing the ball from his hands
- committing any other offence not mentioned in Law 12 for which play is stopped to caution or dismiss a player.

In addition, an indirect free kick is awarded if a goalkeeper, inside his own penalty area, commits any of the following four offences:

- takes more than six seconds while controlling the ball with his hands, before releasing it from his possession
- touches the ball again with his hands after it has been released from his possession and has not touched any other player
- touches the ball with his hands after it has been deliberately kicked to him by a team mate
- touches the ball with his hands after he has received it directly from a throw-in taken by a team mate.

Dangerous play

Dangerous play is generally associated with a player attempting to kick a ball which is sufficiently high for another player to be attempting to head it at the same time. However, there are other actions which the referee may regard as dangerous, and he will penalise the offender for them.

▲ *Fig.12 Dangerous play*

Handling

A player has 'handled the ball' if he has deliberately carried, struck or propelled it with his hand or arm.

It may be impossible for a player to avoid handling the ball, having no time to withdraw his hand or arm before the ball strikes him. Even though he may thus gain advantage, if the offence was not deliberate the referee should not penalise it.

This is vitally important in the penalty area, where a player unable to beat an opponent may decide to kick the ball directly at him, hoping to strike his hand or arm and thus (incorrectly) be awarded a penalty.

▶ *Fig. 13 Charging an opponent*

▶ *Fig. 14 Tripping, using the legs*

Tripping

Tripping is not limited to the use of feet and legs. Some players throw, or try to throw, their opponents by stooping in front of them or even behind them. It is also possible for a player to simulate being tripped by an opponent in order to deceive the referee. Such action will be deemed unsporting behaviour and the guilty player cautioned and shown a yellow card.

Pushing and holding

Contact sports such as soccer inevitably involve the use of hands and arms to maintain balance or for protection.

A player must in no circumstances use his hands or arms either to hold back an opponent or to push him away from the ball. This offence often occurs when the arms of players become interlocked, and the referee must be watchful for such infringements, which may appear 'accidental'.

Even if a player is being unfairly impeded, he may not use his hands to push away an opponent.

Players who try to gain an unfair advantage by holding an opponent's shirt or shorts may be cautioned as well as having a free kick awarded against him, if the referee judged it to be unsporting behaviour.

Jumping at an opponent

A player is penalised for jumping at an opponent. Jumping for the ball, e.g. to head the ball, should not be confused with jumping at an opponent. A player may take a leap to get near the ball.

▲ *Fig. 15   Pushing an opponent*

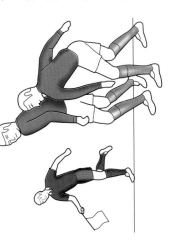

▲ *Fig. 16   Unfair impeding*

without necessarily endangering his opponent.

A fair sliding tackle is not dangerous to either player, especially when clear contact is made with the ball. It should, therefore, not be penalised. Jumping with both feet at the ball when it is being played by an opponent can result in injury, and is therefore penalised.

Unfair impeding

Impeding the progress of an opponent when not attempting to play the ball (e.g. interposing the body so as to form an obstacle to the opponent) is an offence which is penalised by an indirect free kick.

It should not be confused with screening the ball which is natural to the game. A player can shield the ball with his body when he is playing or attempting to play the ball. This is a feature of dribbling and close ball control.

Impeding should also be distinguished from the contact foul (e.g. over-zealously pushing or holding an opponent), which is penalised with a direct free kick (or a penalty kick if the offence is committed in the player's own penalty area).

Misconduct

All spectators enjoy seeing fair and skilful play, unhampered by the use of dishonest tactics to deny goals. Unfortunately, some misguided players occasionally stray from the truly sporting path expected in this game and the referee must then act firmly, fairly and totally impartially to punish appropriately the misdemeanours he has identified.

Among the referee's duties is the cautioning or dismissal of players guilty of misconduct in its various forms. The referee must caution a player and show a yellow card if:

• he enters or re-enters the field of play without the permission of the referee
• he deliberately leaves the field of play without the permission of the referee
• he persistently infringes the laws of the game
• he delays the re-start of play

• he fails to respect the required distance when play is re-started with a corner kick or free kick
• he shows, by word or action, dissent
• he is guilty of unsporting behaviour.

The Laws of the Game now require that, as an outward indication that a player, substitute or a player who has been substituted has been cautioned, the referee holds up a yellow card.

The referee shows a red card and sends the player from the field of play, if:

• he is guilty of violent conduct or serious foul play
• he uses offensive or insulting or abusive language and/or gestures
• he denies the opposing team a goal or an obvious goal-scoring opportunity by deliberately handling the ball (this does not apply to a goalkeeper within his own penalty area)
• he denies an obvious goal-scoring opportunity by an offence punishable by a free kick or penalty kick

• he spits at anyone
• he receives a second caution in the same match.

If a player is sent off for a second cautionable offence in a match, the referee must first show the yellow and then immediately afterwards the red card.

If a player has been sent off, he cannot sit in the technical area and must leave the area around the field of play.

Violent conduct

This occurs when a player is guilty of considerable aggression or violence towards an opponent when they are not challenging for the ball. Also, if a player attacks one of his team mates, the referee, an assistant referee, a spectator or any other person, this is similarly classed as violent conduct.

Serious foul play is recognised in the Laws of the Game as the use of unnecessary or excessive force in unfairly challenging an opponent for the ball.

Goalkeepers

A goalkeeper is a unique player in any team in the sense that he may not only play the ball with his feet like any other player in any part of the field of play, or throw the ball in from the touch line like any other player, but he may also have the privilege of touching the ball with his hands inside his own penalty area. This special privilege, however, means that he has to accept some restrictions in certain circumstances. A goalkeeper needs to be aware of these limitations and the punishments he may incur if he transgresses.

The goalkeeper is considered to be in control of the ball when touching it with any part of his hands or arms. Possession of the ball includes the goalkeeper deliberately parrying the ball, but does not include circumstances where, in the opinion of the referee, the ball rebounds accidentally from the goalkeeper, for example after he has made a save.

However, he must not waste time and has a maximum of 6 seconds to hold the ball before releasing it into play.

Goalkeepers now need to take great care when the ball is deliberately kicked to them by a team mate or thrown directly from a throw-in.

Players should take note that a player who deliberately kicks the ball to his goalkeeper does not commit any offence, but an offence is committed by the goalkeeper at the place where he touches the ball with his hands.

Goalkeepers are therefore advised not to risk handling the ball when it is kicked to them by one of their own team or thrown-in directly to them. It is safer to clear the ball with a foot, the body or the head.

Offside

In most field games in which the main purpose is to score through the opponents' goal, some restrictions are applied to prevent a player waiting in close proximity to the goal, ready to score from short range.

The restricting rule in soccer is known as the offside law, and it provides notable technical features of the game. As the punished infringement of this law results in an immediate breakdown of attack, it is essential that the issue of the law should be clearly grasped in all its details.

It is not an offence in itself for a player to be in an offside position. A player is in an offside position if he is nearer to his opponents' goal line than both the ball and the second last opponent.

A player shall only be penalised for being in an offside position if, at the moment the ball touches, or is played by one of his team, he is, in the opinion of the referee, involved in active play by:

- interfering with play or with an opponent, or
- gaining an advantage by being in that position.

A player is not in an offside position if:

- he is in his own half of the field of play
- he is level with the second last opponent
- he is level with at least two opponents.

There is no offence if a player receives the ball direct from a throw-in, corner kick or goal kick.

For an infringement of the law, an indirect free kick is taken by a player of the opposing team from the place where the infringement occurred (unless the offence is committed by a player in his opponents' goal area, in which case the free kick is taken from anywhere within the goal area).

Example 1

In fig. 17, the ball is touched in its flight by a defending player: attacker 2 is clearly in an offside position and in the active area of play at the moment the ball is played by attacker 1.

An assistant referee should signal as soon as attacker 1 plays the ball that attacker 2 has committed an offside offence.

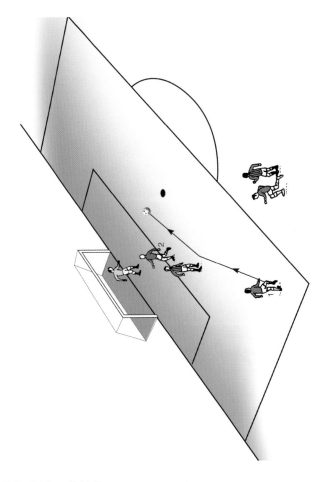

Fig.17 Offside: example 1 ▲

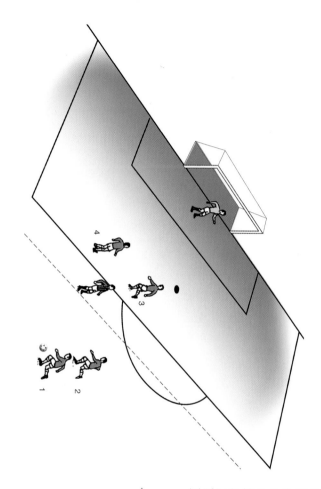

Example 2

In fig. 18, attackers 2, 3 and 4 are all nearer to their opponents' goal line than the ball is: they are in potentially offside positions. At the moment attacker 1 plays the ball, attackers 3 and 4 may become offside (since there is only one opponent between them and the defenders' goal line). Attacker 2 is onside (there are two opponents between him and the opponents' goal line).

▲ *Fig.18 Offside: example 2*

Example 3

In fig. 19, attackers 2 and 3 cannot be offside direct from a corner kick (i.e. when the kick is taken). If, however, the ball goes direct from the corner kick to attacker 2 who then plays it to attacker 3, the latter is then penalised for an offside offence. The same principle applies to a throw-in, or a goal kick.

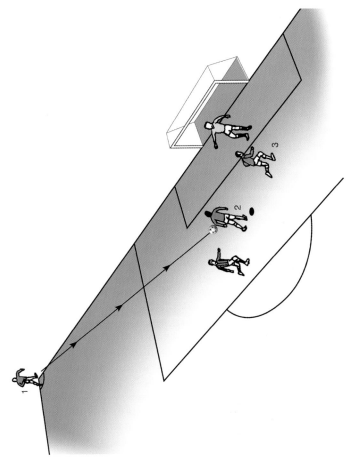

Fig.19 Offside: example 3 ▲

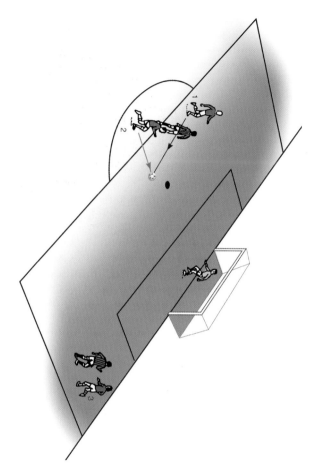

Example 4

In fig. 20, attacker 1 passes to attacker 2. It might be argued that attacker 3, who is in an offside position, is so far away from the play that he is not interfering. However, he may be doing so indirectly by distracting the defender from covering attacker 2. The referee must decide quickly whether or not, in his opinion, attacker 3 is involved in active play and interfering with play or the opponent.

▲ *Fig. 20 Offside: example 4*

Question 1

Attacker 1 in fig. 21 takes a corner kick; it goes to attacker 2, who shoots, but attacker 3 deflects it into goal. What is the decision?

Attacker 2 is not offside direct from the corner kick, but attacker 3 is involved in active play and in an offside position when attacker 2 passes the ball to him. Attacker 3 is nearer the goal line than the ball is, and has only one defender – the goalkeeper – between him and the goal line when the ball is played by attacker 2.

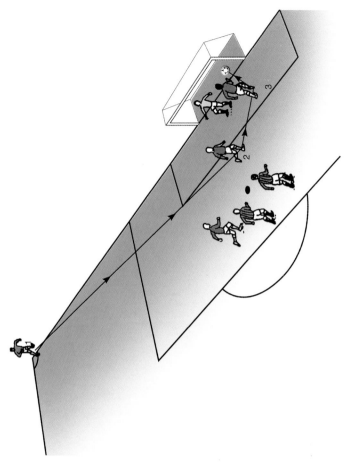

Fig.21 Offside: question 1 ▲

Question 2

Attacker 1 in fig. 22, who has beaten the defender, passes to attacker 2, who scores. What is the decision?

Attacker 2 is not offside when attacker 1 plays the ball, for at this moment he is not in front of the ball. Thus a goal is awarded.

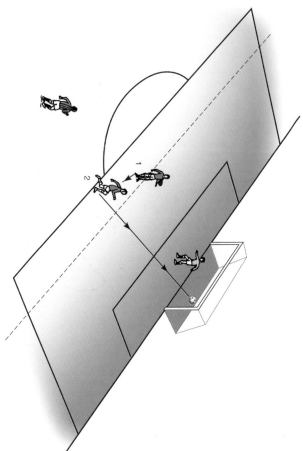

▲ *Fig. 22 Offside: question 2*

Question 3

Attacker 1 in fig. 23 takes a throw-in;
the ball goes to attacker 2, who passes
it to attacker 3, who scores. What is
the decision?

Attacker 2 cannot be offside from
the throw-in, and when the ball is
passed to him, attacker 3 is not nearer
to the goal line than the ball is. A goal
is awarded.

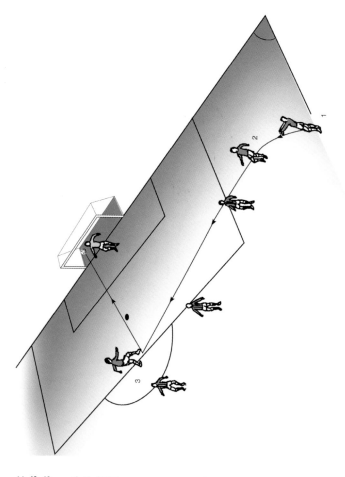

Fig.23 Offside: question 3 ▲

Question 4

Attacker 1 in fig. 24, who has dribbled past the defender, shoots; the ball rebounds off the goal post (red line) or is fisted by the goalkeeper (blue line) to attacker 2, who scores. What is the decision?

Attacker 2 is not offside from the rebound, since he is not in front of the ball when it is played by attacker 1. Therefore it is a goal, unless the referee adjudges that attacker 1, who is in an offside position, is also involved in active play and is interfering with play when attacker 2 shoots.

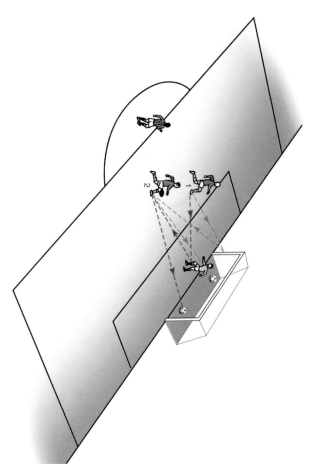

▲ Fig.24 Offside: question 4

Free kicks

There are two types of free kick:

- indirect – from which a goal cannot be scored without the ball touching another player
- direct – from which a goal can be scored direct against the offending side.

The ten offences for which a direct free kick is awarded are listed on page 20.

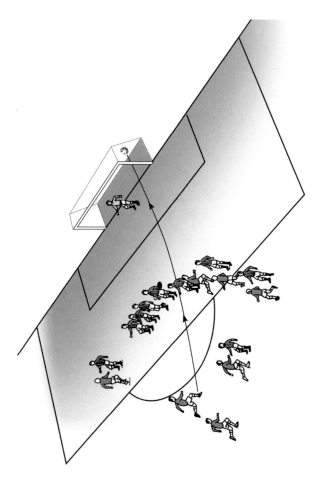

Fig.25 Direct free kick ▲

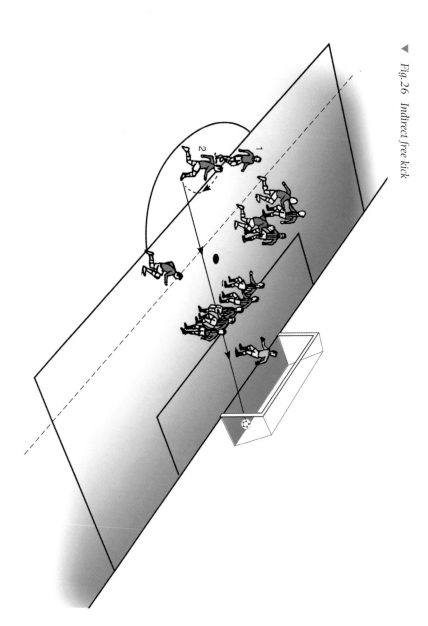

▼ Fig.26 Indirect free kick

Free kick inside own penalty area

All opposing players must be at least 9.15 m (10 yds) from the ball, and must remain outside the penalty area until the ball has been kicked out of the area.

The ball is in play immediately it has been kicked and moves beyond the penalty area. If the ball is not kicked directly into play beyond the penalty area, the kick is re-taken. The goal-keeper must not receive the ball into his hands so that he can kick it into play.

If the free kick is to be taken in the goal area, the ball may be placed at any point within the goal area in which the offence occurred.

Free kick outside own penalty area

The kick is taken from the place where the infringement occurred, subject to the special circumstances described on page 18. All players of the offending side must be at least 9.15 m (10 yds) from the ball until it is in play.

The ball must be stationary when a free kick is taken, and is in play when it has been kicked and moves.

If, after taking a free kick, the kicker plays the ball a second time before it touches another player, his opponents are awarded an indirect free kick from where the offence occurred.

Penalty kick

A penalty kick is awarded for any one of the ten offences listed on page 20 committed by a defending player in his own penalty area (except when a goal-keeper handles the ball).

The penalty kick is taken from the penalty mark, 11 m (12 yds) from the mid-point of the goal line. All players, other than the goalkeeper and the player taking the kick, must be:

- on the field of play
- outside the penalty area
- at least 9.15 m (10 yds) from the ball
- behind the penalty mark until the kick has been taken.

The goalkeeper must remain on his goal line between the goal posts until the ball has been kicked by the player taking the penalty kick. He may move along his goal line, but not off his goal line towards the kicker. The player must kick the ball forwards, and cannot play the ball a second time until it has touched or been played by another player. The ball is in play as soon as it has been kicked and moves forward.

A goal may be scored direct from a penalty kick; a goal is also allowed if the ball touches either or both goal posts, the cross-bar, the goalkeeper or any combination of these before passing between the posts and under the cross-bar.

If necessary, play is continued at half-time or full time to allow the penalty kick to be properly taken; this also applies to either half of extra time.

Infringements at the penalty kick

For any infringement by the defending side at the taking of the penalty kick:

- if a goal is scored, it is allowed
- if no goal is scored, the kick is re-taken.

For any infringement by the attacking team, other than the player taking the kick:

- if a goal is scored, it must be disallowed and the kick re-taken
- if no goal is scored, the kick is not re-taken.

For any infringement by the player taking the kick, after the ball is in play (e.g. playing the ball a second time without it having touched another player), an opponent takes an indirect free kick from the place where the infringement occurred, subject to the special circumstances described on page 18.

Question 1

Attacker 1 is taking a penalty kick, but before he reaches the ball, attacker 2 runs over the 9.15 m (10 yds) penalty arc line. What is the decision?

Attacker 2 commits an offence. Therefore, if attacker 1 kicks the ball into goal from the penalty kick, the referee orders the kick to be re-taken; if the kicker does not put the ball into goal, the kick is not re-taken.

Question 2

An attacker takes a penalty kick, but as the ball enters the goal, a defender runs into the penalty area. What is the decision?

Regardless of whether the defender moves before or after the ball is kicked, if it goes into the goal, a goal is scored.

Question 3

Attacker 1 takes a penalty kick and the ball strikes the upright and rebounds to attacker 2: he runs in and scores. What is the decision?

Attacker 2 is not offside and does not move forwards into the penalty area until attacker 1 has taken the kick, so a goal is scored. If attacker 1 is in front of attacker 2 when the latter shoots, the referee might adjudge him to be involved in active play and interfering with play, and give him offside.

Question 4

Additional time is being allowed for a penalty kick. An attacker takes the kick, which is punched out by the goalkeeper. The same attacker follows up and kicks the ball into goal. What is the decision?

Additional time is allowed for the penalty kick only. As the goalkeeper saves the kick, the referee signals for full time and no goal is scored.

Control of the game

The four officials responsible for the control of a game of soccer are:

- an appointed referee, who has primary responsibility, and who controls the game on the field of play, and
- two assistant referees (one for each touch line)
- a stand-by or fourth official.

The laws make no stipulation concerning the dress of the officials, but it is customary to wear kit that is clearly distinctive from that of the players, particularly in the case of socks and shirt.

Referees and assistant referees are advised to consult the rules of the competition in which they officiate. The referee in particular needs to be aware of possible variations regarding the ball, extra time, duration of play, length of half-time interval, etc.

Referee

Each match is controlled by a referee who has full authority to enforce the Laws of the Game in connection with the match to which he has been appointed.

The referee should have two good whistles, two reliable watches, a coin, a notebook, a yellow and a red card, and a pencil.

On points of fact connected with play, the referee's decision is final as far as the result of the game is concerned. His authority, and the exercise of the powers granted to him by the Laws of the Game, commence as soon as he enters the field of play (and continue if play is temporarily suspended).

Although he may have two assistant referees to assist him, the referee has the sole responsibility for enforcing the Laws of the Game. He must know not only the Laws, but also their correct interpretation and application.

Powers and duties

The referee:

- enforces the Laws of the Game
- controls the match in co-operation with the assistant referees and, where applicable, with the fourth official
- ensures that the ball meets the requirements of Law 2
- ensures that the players' equipment meets the requirements of Law 4
- acts as timekeeper and keeps a record of the match
- stops, suspends or terminates the match, at his discretion, for any infringements of the Laws
- stops, suspends or terminates the match because of outside interference of any kind
- stops the match if, in his opinion, a player is seriously injured and ensures that he is removed from the field of play
- allows play to continue until the ball is out of play if a player is, in his opinion, only slightly injured
- ensures that any player bleeding from a wound leaves the field of play. The player may only return on receiving a

signal from the referee, who must be satisfied that the bleeding has stopped

- allows play to continue when the team against which an offence has been committed will benefit from such an advantage, and penalises the original offence if the anticipated advantage does not ensue at that time
- punishes the more serious offence when a player commits more than one offence at the same time
- takes disciplinary action against players guilty of cautionable and sending-off offences. He is not obliged to take this action immediately but must do so when the ball next goes out of play
- takes action against team officials who fail to conduct themselves in a responsible manner and may, at his discretion, expel them from the field of play and its immediate surrounds
- acts on the advice of assistant referees regarding incidents which he has not seen
- ensures that no unauthorised persons enter the field of play
- restarts the match after it has stopped

• provides the appropriate authorities with a match report which includes information on any disciplinary action taken against players, and/or team officials and any other incidents which occurred before, during or after the match.

Assistant referee

Duties

Two assistant referees are appointed whose duties, subject to the decision of the referee, are to indicate:

• when the whole of the ball has passed out of the field of play
• which side is entitled to a corner kick, goal kick or throw-in
• when a player may be penalised for being in an offside position
• when a substitution is requested
• when misconduct or any other incident has occurred out of the view of the referee
• when offences have been committed whenever the assistants are closer to the action than the referee (this

includes, in particular circumstances, offences committed in the penalty area)
• whether, at penalty kicks, the goalkeeper has moved forward before the ball has been kicked, and whether the ball has crossed the line.

Assistance

The assistant referees also assist the referee to control the match in accordance with the Laws of the Game. In particular, they may enter the field of play to help control the 9.15 m distance.

In the event of undue interference or improper conduct, the referee will relieve an assistant referee of his duties and make a report to the appropriate authorities.

The flags used by assistant referees should be of different colours, and are usually provided by the home club. Experience has proved that orange-yellow and flame red are good colours for flags. The assistant referee should always carry his flag unfurled so that his signals will be clearly seen.

The fourth official

The fourth official is a qualified referee who is available to replace one of the other officials who may become injured. In addition, he has a range of other duties. He can:

• assist with substitutions
• supervise behaviour in the technical areas
• indicate how much time the referee has allowed for stoppages.

He also reports to the referee any serious misconduct which may have happened outside the view of the other match officials.

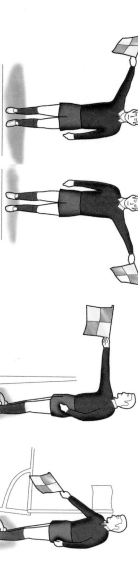

▶ Figs 27 and 28 Throw-in (to the side playing in the direction of the flag)

▶ Fig.29 Goal kick

▶ Fig.30 Corner kick

▶ Fig.31 Offside on far side

▶ Fig.32 Offside in a roughly central position

▶ Fig.33 Offside on the assistant referee's side of the field

▶ Fig.34 Substitution

▶ Fig.35 Advising the award of a penalty kick

▶ Fig.36 Indicating that on his watch the 45 minutes of the half are completed

Diagonal system of control

The diagonal system of control is designed to cover the whole of the field of play by co-operative effort between the referee and the two assistant referees.

The assistant referees are positioned to cover each half of the field, and therefore to be up with play to judge offside offences. One aspect of the offside law involves the alignment of players, which is only accurately judged by a view of play at right angles to the touch line. Assistant referees are better prepared for judging such offences if their patrol is limited to approximately half of the touch line.

In diagonal patrol, the referee moves so that if play changes rapidly from wing to wing he is covered by one of the assistant referees (see fig. 37).

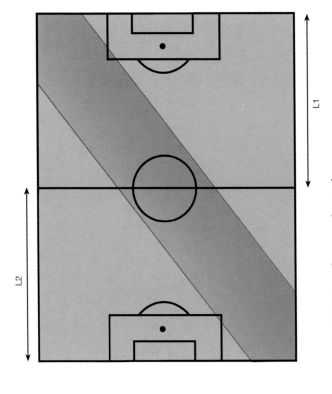

▲ *Fig. 37 Diagonal system of control*

While the assistant referees may assist the referee, it is usual for the latter to judge all infringements of play other than the ball out of play and offside. If a referee rigidly adopts the diagonal system, he may be too far away to give an accurate assessment, or, when the atmosphere of play demands, to exercise adequate control.

It is advisable for the referee to keep reasonably close to the play at all times by using a wide diagonal zone as shown in fig. 37. This avoids the possibility of having two officials at the same spot, and also allows the referee to move sideways when the position of play demands it.

Modifications

School soccer

Subject to the approval of national associations, and provided the principles of the Laws are maintained, the following modifications may be made for schoolchildren up to 16 years of age:

- the size of the field of play
- the size, weight and material of the ball
- the width between the goal posts and the height of the cross-bar from the ground
- the duration of the periods of play
- substitutions.

Women's soccer

As with schoolchildren, the Laws can be modified providing the principles are adhered to in the five areas outlined.

These modifications are now also accepted for veterans' soccer competitions, for players with disabilities, and approved by the national association.

Further modifications are permissible only with the consent of the International Board.

The Football Association

THE FOOTBALL ASSOCIATION

Information regarding national, regional and local courses, together with addresses of county coaching secretaries, may be obtained from:

The Football Association
25 Soho Square
London W1D 4FA

Index

advantage law 43
area
  goal 11
  penalty 10, 39
assistant referees 41–6

ball 5
  out of play 16–19
boots 4
boundary line 8

captain 13
caution 24
centre circle 8
corner kick 19
cross-bar 11, 14
cycling shorts 2

dangerous play 21
diagonal system of control 45
dismissal 24
dissent 24
dropped ball 31

end, choice of 13
extra time 13

field of play 6–12
flag post 11
Football Association, The 47
foul play, serious 24
fourth official 41–3
free kicks 20–1, 37–9

goal 11–12
  area 11
  kick 18
  line 8
  post 11
goalkeeper 2–3, 26
Golden Goal 15

half-time 13
halfway line 8
handling 22
holding 23

impeding 23

jumping 23

kick
  corner 19
  direct free 20, 37
  free 20–1, 37–9
  goal 18
  indirect free 21, 37–8
  -off 13
  penalty 40–1

misconduct 24

nets 11

offences 20–36
officials 41–6
offside 28–36

penalty
  arc 10
  area 10, 39
  kick 15, 40–1
  mark 10
pushing 23

referee 41–3

school soccer 46
scoring 14
shielding 23
shin guards 2–3
shirt 2–3
shorts 2–3
socks 2–3
substitution 14

technical area 9
throw-in 17
time wasting 13
toss 13
touch line 8
tripping 22

unsporting behaviour 23–4

violent conduct 24

women's soccer 46

48